MACK® MODEL C FIRE TRUCKS
1957 THROUGH 1967

PHOTO ARCHIVE

Edited with introduction by
Harvey Eckart

Iconografix
Photo Archive Series

Iconografix
PO Box 446
Hudson, Wisconsin 54016 USA

Library of Congress Card Number: 99-76043

ISBN 1-58388-014-3

00 01 02 03 04 05 06 5 4 3 2 1

Printed in the United States of America

Cover and book design by Shawn Glidden

Copy Editing by Dylan Frautschi

Iconografix Inc. exists to preserve history through the publication of notable photographic archives and the list of titles under the Iconografix imprint is constantly growing. Transportation enthusiasts should be on the Iconografix mailing list and are invited to write and ask for a catalog, free of charge.

Authors and editors in the field of transportation history are invited to contact the Editorial Department at Iconografix, Inc., PO Box 446, Hudson, WI 54016. We require a minimum of 120 photographs per subject. We prefer subjects narrow in focus, e.g., a specific model, railroad, or racing venue. Photographs must be of high-quality, suited to large format reproduction.

PREFACE

The histories of machines and mechanical gadgets are contained in the books, journals, correspondence, and personal papers stored in libraries and archives throughout the world. Written in tens of languages, covering thousands of subjects, the stories are recorded in millions of words.

Words are powerful. Yet, the impact of a single image, a photograph or an illustration, often relates more than dozens of pages of text. Fortunately, many of the libraries and archives that house the words also preserve the images.

In the *Photo Archive Series,* Iconografix reproduces photographs and illustrations selected from public and private collections. The images are chosen to tell a story—to capture the character of their subject. Reproduced as found, they are accompanied by the captions made available by the archive.

The Iconografix *Photo Archive Series* is dedicated to young and old alike, the enthusiast, the collector and anyone who, like us, is fascinated by "things" mechanical.

ACKNOWLEDGMENTS

The photographs appearing in this book were made available by the Mack Trucks Historical Museum and the private collection of the author.

BIBLIOGRAPHY

Sytsma, John, AHRENS-FOX ALBUM 1973

Montville, John B., MACK, Aztec Corporation, Tucson, AZ 1979

Calderone, John A and Jack Lerch, WHEELS OF THE BRAVEST 1865 - 1982 Fire Apparatus Journal Publications, Inc. Howard Beach
New York. 1984

Ahrens Fox Fire Buff Assn., THE SILVER SPHERE VOL 5, NO. 13 1989

Eckart, Harvey, MACK FIRE APPARATUS, A PICTORIAL HISTORY. The Engine House, Middletown, New York 1990

Eckart, Harvey, LAST OF THE BREED The Engine House, Middletown, New York 1994

The very first C models delivered by Mack were two C85 pumpers to Providence, RI, in November 1957. One of these pieces is shown about to respond on a call.

INTRODUCTION

In the fall of 1954 Mack introduced the B model conventional type fire apparatus, which replaced both the popular A and L series. At this point in time Mack did not have a cab-forward type apparatus to compete with archrival American LaFrance, who introduced the post WWII cab-forward style to the fire service in 1945. Crown Body & Coach Corp. in California introduced their first custom fire apparatus in 1951, also utilizing the cab-forward design exclusively. Ahrens-Fox, which was suffering a slow, painful financial death, was sold to General Truck Sales Corp. of Cincinnati, OH, in 1951, who contracted the actual construction of Ahrens-Fox apparatus to the C. D. Beck Company of Sidney, OH, in 1953. Beck was a small builder of buses. Renowned Ahrens-Fox salesman Frank Griesser and Beck engineers and designers created a new Ahrens-Fox cab-forward series, called ECB and FCB models in 1956. Six of these were built by Beck after acquiring exclusive rights to manufacture all Ahrens-Fox apparatus in 1955.

In September 1956 Mack bought the C. D. Beck Company for the purpose of building inter-city buses, in anticipation of a large contract that did not materialize. Mack engineers were impressed with the Ahrens-Fox cab-forward design, and almost as an afterthought, Mack purchased the production rights to the Ahrens-Fox cab-forward design. This proved to be a favorable decision, and in 1957 Mack began producing C model apparatus at the Sidney plant, as well as B model apparatus assembly, transferred from the Pennsylvania facilities. In addition, Mack produced the inter-city bus model 97D (also based on a Beck design) at the Sidney plant.

Mack bus production on the 97D diminished quickly at the Sidney plant with only twenty-six built in 1958. The C model fire apparatus line was an entirely different story as 1,055 were produced over the next eleven years until replaced by the CF series in late 1967. Fire apparatus production of both the B and C series was returned to Pennsylvania after closure of the Sidney plant in December 1958. Hahn Motors in Hamburg, PA, assembled Mack apparatus for a short time, before all production was again returned to the Mack Allentown facilities.

Although a latecomer in the cab-forward market and not an original Mack design, the C model Mack was an instant success and became a major market contender. The C model design was and is one of the best, if not THE best looking cab-forward apparatus ever built, then or now.

Pumpers comprised the bulk of C model deliveries, but straight frame and tillered aerial in 65, 75, 85, and 100 foot lengths were also popular. A significant development involving the C series was the introduction in 1964 of one of the first telescoping aerial platforms, called the Aerialscope, of 75 foot length. The C and CF Mack Aerialscopes were the almost exclusive aerial platform type apparatus in the New York City Fire Department for over thirty years.

Like the companion B model, the C model was a transitional series. It was available in both semi-open and closed canopy cabs. The 464, 540, and 707 gasoline motors were standard, with the 707C being the most popular. After 1960, Mack offered a diesel motor, which slowly but surely began to replace the gasoline motor in popularity. Both hydraulic and air brakes were offered, and in 1960 Waterous replaced Hale as the standard pump brand. Pump sizes ranged from 500 to 1250 GPM with larger sizes available on a special order basis.

The C model was built to conform to the minimum performance and equipment requirements specified by the National Fire Protection Association (NFPA), but a staggering array of optional equipment was available. The photos to follow are arranged by serial number in chronological order (for the most part), by types, and illustrate the wide variety and diversity of C units. Captions list many optional and non-standard features.

Today, over thirty years since C model production ended, many are still answering fire calls. A great many out-of-service rigs are now owned by collectors and fire companies, who have restored them to like-new condition for future generations to enjoy. The C model is truly one of Mack's "crowning achievements" in the fire apparatus field.

C-85F • C-95F • C-125F TRIPLE COMBINATION PUMPERS

(2) CORNER STEPS (ONE (EACH SIDE) OF ENGINE COMPARTMENT

(4) 6 VOLT 120 AMP. BATTERIES MTD. IN COMPT. R.H. SIDE

RADIO COMPT. UNDER R.H. CAB SEAT

WINDSHIELD WIPERS (OUTSIDE VAC.)

SLIDING GLASS PARTITION IN CAB

CHROME PLATED FRONT BUMPER WITH ALUMINUM STEP PLATE

118

71 3/4

20

96

PARTITION

8

(2) REAR VIEW MIRRORS (ONE EACH SIDE) WITH BRACES

TOOL COMPT. L.H. SIDE. APPROX. SIZE: 29L. X 15W. X 11H.

PRESSURE VOLUME CENTRIFUGAL PUMP.

FILLER SPOUT (SPRING TYPE CAP) FOR BOOSTER TANK. WITH REMOVE-ABLE COVER (10 GA. MATERIAL) (300 GAL. TANK SHOWN)

SIREN WITH STEER-ING COLUMN BUTTON AND RIGHT HAND SWITCH CONTROL.

HANDRAIL MTD. TOP OF FIREWALL

(1.) PUMP PRESSURE GA.
(1.) PUMP COMPOUND GA.
(1.) ENGINE TACHOMETER.
(1.) WATER LEVEL GA.
(1.) ENGINE TEMP. GA.
(1.) OIL PRESSURE GA.

TOP MTD. MANUAL REWIND HOSE REEL WITH 200' OF 1" BOOSTER HOSE.

(2) HOSE BODY LIGHTS

RELIEF VALVE CONTROL
10 FT. PIKE POLE

(2) HANDRAILS ONE EACH SIDE.

(2) UNITY LIGHTS.

110 APPROX. HEIGHT.

(2) FRONT DIRECTIONAL SIGNALS.

(2) REAR DIRECTIONAL SIGNALS.

A

TOP OF FRAME

18

(2) STOP AND TAIL LIGHTS.

16

INTERMEDIATE CORNER STEP

(2) CHARGING PLUGS

Ȼ CHASSIS

(2) TOWING EYES

9.00-20 12 PLY SINGLE

86

900-20 12 PLY (DUAL)

FILLER FOR 41 GAL. FUEL TANK.

80

66 13/16

160

(4) RIGIDIZED ALUMINUM KICKPLATES (2 EACH SIDE)

306 13/16

FULL LENGTH COMPTS. APPROXIMATE SIZES:
2- COMPTS, ONE EACH SIDE, FRONT OF REAR WHEELS. COMPT. SIZE: 32 X 24D X 28W-DOOR OPENING 28H X 27W.
2- COMPTS, ONE EACH SIDE, REAR OF REAR WHEELS. COMPT. SIZE: 32 X 24D X 32W-DOOR OPENING: 28H X 27W.

REAR COMPT. APPROX. SIZE: 30W. X 32H X 22D. DOOR OPENING: 27W. X 28H.

NOTE: ALL DOORS ARE WEATHERPROOF

TANK	A HOSE BODY HEIGHT	2 1/2 HOSE CAPACITY	1 1/2 HOSE CAPACITY
300 GAL. FLAT	38	1400	500
500 GAL. FLAT	40	1200	500

STANDARD EQUIPMENT

Conventional and Cab-forward TRIPLE COMBINATION PUMPERS

SUCTION HOSE: 2—10′ Hard Rubber

LADDERS (WOOD): 1—24′ Solid Side Extension. 1—14′ Roof, with folding hooks

LIGHTING EQUIPMENT: Sealed beam headlights: 2 on conventional Model. 4 on cab-forward
Directional signals — front and rear red parking lights
2 combination stop and tail lights
License plate bracket with light
2 hose body lights, 2 front spotlights, 2 motor lights over pump gauges
Instrument panel lights
Automatic lights in compartments (5)

PUMP: 2-stage centrifugal, rotary gear primer pump. Master drain on operator's panel. 2½″ gated side suction. Quarter-turn valve in all water lines.

BOOSTER TANK: 300 gal. capacity

COMPARTMENTS: 4 running board and one rear, 1 radio compartment in cab skirting, right side on Conventional model
1 compartment in step to rear seat on left and 1 radio compartment under officer's seat on Cab-forward Model

TOWING EYES: 2 front—2 rear on "C" Model—2 tow hooks front and 2 tow eyes rear on Conventional Model

WARNING SIGNALS: 360° Revolving light on cab
One siren with grille—One electric horn

PIKE POLE: 1—10 foot

AXES: 1 flat head; 1 pick-back

MOUNTINGS: 2 playpipe cones or screwbases

CROWBAR: 1—50″

HAND LANTERNS: 2 Electric

SUCTION STRAINER: Barrel type

HYDRANT CONNECTIONS: One 4½″ x 2½″, one 4½″ x large hydrant

HOSE CONNECTIONS: 1—2½″ double male 1—2½″ double female

HOSE REEL: Top mounted

BOOSTER HOSE: 200′ of 1″—1 combination fog and straight stream nozzle

HOSE BODY CAPACITY: 1400′—2½″ 500′—1½″

PUMP PANEL GAUGES: Master pump pressure, Compound gauge, Tachometer and engine hour meter, Oil pressure gauge, temperature gauge, Booster tank level gauge

EXTINGUISHERS: 1—20 lb. dry chemical—1—2½ gallon foam

MACK TRIPLE COMBINATION PUMPERS

CONVENTIONAL MODELS					**SPECIFICATIONS Standard Apparatus**	CAB FORWARD MODELS				
B505F	B75F	B85F	B95F	B125F		C505F	C75F	C85F	C95F	C125F
500	750	750	1000	1250	RATED CAPACITY (GPM)	500	750	750	1000	1250
168½″ 282″ 96″ 103″					**DIMENSIONS:** Wheelbase Overall length Overall width Overall Height (top of light)	160″ 307″ 96″ 110″				
ENF 540 4 9/16″ x 5½″ 540 cu. in. 204 @ 2800 RPM 460 lb. ft.	ENF 707C 5″ x 6″ 707 cu. in. 276 @ 2600 RPM 640 lb. ft.				**ENGINE:** **Mack** Thermodyne Six Cylinder, overhead Bore and stroke Piston Displacement Maximum horsepower Maximum torque @ 1400 RPM By-pass Lube oil filter, 2 qts.	ENF 540 4 9/16″ x 5½″ 540 cu. in 204 @ 2800 RPM 460 lb. ft.	ENF 707C 5″ x 6″ 707 cu. in. 276 @ 2600 RPM 640 lb. ft.			
Updraft	Dual downdraft				**FUEL SYSTEM:** Zenith Carburetor 41 gallon tank, in rear	Updraft	Dual downdraft			
All Models					**COOLING SYSTEM:** Auxiliary cooling — Pump water through copper coil in unit in thermostatically controlled by-pass system	All Models				
"					**ELECTRIC SYSTEM:** 12V. 100 amp alternator—Dual ignition	"				
"					**CLUTCH:** **Mack** with Vibrasorb clutch plate Type: Single plate, dry	"				
"					**TRANSMISSION:** **Mack,** Five speed Selective, constant mesh	"				
"					**FRONT AXLE:** **Mack,** Reversed Elliott, I Beam	"				
"					**REAR AXLE:** **Mack,** Single Reduction	"				
Front size, 15″ x 2½″ x 5/16″ (166)					**BRAKES:** Vacuum-Hydraulic Rear, 16″ x 6″ x 3/8″ (406) Hand, 12″ x 5″ x 3/8″ (139)	16″ x 4″ x 3/8″ (270)				
All Models					**FRAME:** Chrome manganese, heat treated	All Models				
"					**WHEELS:** Steel casting, six spokes	"				
9:00 x 20 (10 ply)					**TIRES:** Rims: 7.0	9:00 x 20 (12 ply)				
All Models					**STEERING GEAR:** Worm and Roller type Steering wheel, diameter—22″	All Models				
4½″	4½″	4½″	5″	6″	**SUCTION HOSE**	4½″	4½″	4½″	5″	6″
Coupe—3 man					**TYPE OF CAB**	Canopy—5 man				

Standard pumper chassis and fire equipment, as shown from this 1961 sales brochure.

Both B and C model Mack fire apparatus were assembled in 1957 and 1958 at the former C. D. Beck Company plant in Sidney, OH. This aerial view was taken in February 1958. This 200,000-square-foot plant was used for both bus and fire apparatus design and production.

The Sidney plant was a beehive of activity as the first order of FDNY pumpers was under construction in 1957. A lone bus is shown in the left of the photo.

Shown undergoing pump tests at Sidney are a B model semi-cab for Spring Garden Township, York, PA, a canopy cab FDNY C model, and an unidentified B model deluxe cab pumper.

This 1964 photo of plant 4 in Allentown, PA, shows the fire line after its return to PA, following the sale of the Sidney, OH, plant in 1958.

TYPES 505, 75, & 21

The type 505, with a 500 GPM pump was a dying breed by 1957, and only two C505s were built, one in 1960 and one in 1962. A small ENF464A or ENF540 thermodyne gasoline motor were offered.

The type 75 was equipped with a 750 GPM pump, but only offered the smaller ENF464A or ENF540 motors. Only six C75s were produced. The first (C75F1002) was delivered to Lakewood, OH, on January 23, 1958 and the last (C75F1007) was delivered to Bloomingdale, NJ, on July 10, 1962.

The type 21 was also an "endangered species." The type 21 was offered with a large Hall Scott gasoline motor and a 1000 GPM or larger pump. Most Hall Scott motors were specified by West Coast departments and the C21F was no exception. Five (serial numbers C21F1001 through 5) were delivered to Los Angeles, CA, Fire Dept. in 1958.

C505F1000-560-F8252

C505F1000 1960 - The first and only type 505 pumper was for export to Cuba. It was assembled by Hahn Motors in Hamburg, PA, and was equipped with a 500 GPM pump and an ENF540 motor, which developed 204 HP at 2800 RPM, and 460 foot pounds of torque at 1400 RPM. The only other type 505 built was a C505F1001 chassis, which was delivered to N. Massapequa, NY, with a Gerstenslager bodied floodlight unit in 1963.

C75F1004 1959 - The third of six C75s built was this canopy cab pumper. The delivery record shows Mt. View, NJ, but Wayne, NJ, is the lettering on the unit. This pumper was powered by the smallest motor offered, an ENF464B, which developed 200 HP at 3100 RPM, and 395 foot pounds of torque at 1600 RPM. A Hale QL75 HD pump was used.

C21F1001/5 1958 - Five semi-cabs for Los Angeles, CA, were equipped with Hale ZMPHD 1250 pumps and Hall Scott 6156-G-1 motors. These 935-cubic-inch, dual ignition motors developed 300 HP at 2400 RPM. Disc wheels, front suction, and a large deck pipe with pump panel Siamese connections were prominent. LA City and LA County Fire Departments operated the largest Hall Scott powered fleets in the country.

Cab Forward

Completely Mack built, modern, functional and progressive in engineering, the standard Mack fire apparatus is available in standard canopy or semi-cab styles. A feature of the cab-forward type is a double front bumper which affords additional protection to occupants in the event of a front end collision. The rear section of the canopy is sturdily constructed, removable, and will support a 1250 gpm deluge gun in action.

Standard C model canopy cab pumper equipment and configuration are shown, from a 1959 sales brochure. Mack touted the fact they built both cab-forward and conventional apparatus, and manufactured their own major components.

Sales literature from 1961 presents cab-forward features and construction.

CAB FORWARD

In this cab, which is for cab forward apparatus, attractive lines and styling are combined with sturdy construction without compromise. This Mack cab is an all-steel, welded fabrication with square-section tubular framing. Fastenings secure the cab firmly but with a resiliency that alleviates vibration and strains.

Comfortable seating for five is provided, three seats in front and two, facing rearward, in the rear position of the cab and there is a sliding glass partition. The driver's seat is adjustable to suit differently proportioned drivers.

The cab is entirely proof against weather and fumes, it is roomy, visibility is excellent and controls and all instruments are in convenient arrangeemnt. The interior and its appointments while attractive are of practical and durable character. There is ample provision for ventilation. Door windows are regulation type and there is a sliding rear window.

Easy accessibility to the engine is afforded, instruments can be readily tended, accessory items are conveniently accommodated and the door window mechanism and glass are quickly removable with the door inside panel.

Practical in design, staunchly built and nicely fashioned, the cab enjoys an excellent reputation of popularity.

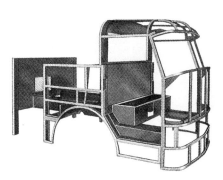

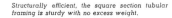

Structurally efficient, the square section tubular framing is sturdy with no excess weight.

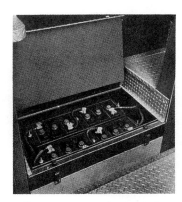

Easy access encourages the appropriately periodic attention to batteries.

MACK TRUCKS, INC. • Plainfield, N. J.
FIRE APPARATUS DIVISION, ALLENTOWN, PA.

TYPE 85

Type 85s were produced from 1957 through 1967 with 308 built. The first two, serial numbers C85F1001 and 2 were delivered to Providence, RI, in November 1957. The last type 85 (C85FD1437) was delivered to Boulevard Heights, MD, on June 13, 1968.

The type 85 was initially equipped with a 707B motor and was soon followed by a 707C motor, which was Mack's premium and largest gasoline offering. Both were 707-cubic-inch overhead valve thermodyne motors with dual ignition. After 1960, an ENDTF673 diesel motor became an option, and slowly began to overshadow the 707C.

A 750 GPM Hale, two stage, centrifugal pump was initially the standard pump, which was replaced by the Waterous brand after 1960.

C85F1001/2 1957 - The very first C models for Providence, RI, were rather plain. Front lighting consisted of dual headlights, bumper mounted turn signals, red parking lights, and red roof mounted siren light. Disc wheels and painted mirrors are shown.

C85F1001/2 - Shown in this plant shot are the center mounted bell and lack of running board compartments.

C85F1001/2 - The Beck bus heritage is evident in these front end shots of both the C85 pumper and the 97D bus.

C85F1003/45 1957 - The first major fleet order of C85s went to New York City. Many detailed photos of these early units were taken. This photo shows the cab framing of one-inch square steel tubing, which comprises the skeleton for the cab sheeting.

C85F1003/45 - The cab sheeting is now in place.

C.1059E 2730

This 1959 photo shows a cab with glass installed and initial emblems and trim applied.

C85F1003/45 - FDNY specs called for canopy roof mounted deluge gun, door reflectors, "subway strap" grab handles, center mounted rear discharge booster reel, and small side mounted grab handles.

C85F1003/45 - Pump panel details show individual pressure gauges, electric tachometer, gated 2 1/2-inch inlet, master drain valve, Hale relief and power operated transfer valves, and Ross intake relief valve.

C85F1003/45 - Front end details include single headlights, red parking lights, 6 inch red lights, roof mounted siren, small air horns, Federal rotating beacon light, center mounted spotlight, and painted bumper and mirrors.

C85F1046 1957 - Of the fifty-two C85s delivered to FDNY in 1958, this one was delivered with a torque converter and had a chrome bumper to differentiate it from its manual transmission brothers. Minor changes from the photo on page 27 include chrome mirrors, large grab handles, and a lack of reflectors on the front panel and doors.

C85F1046 - Right and rear view shows gated rear intakes, larger tail and stop lights, soft suction hose, CO_2 extinguisher, and odd mounting of hydrant adapters on body instead of running board.

C85F1046 - The 707B motor was equipped with a dual downdraft carburetor and polished valve covers. It produced 225 HP at 2600 RPM and 579 foot pounds of torque at 1100 RPM. The 707B had six spark plugs on each side of the motor, whereas the later 707C had all twelve on one side.

C85F1046 - Dual rear mounted 2 1/2-inch intakes were located on the left and the large non-gated inlet was on the right rear.

C85F1046 - Details of the steering column and radiator placement are shown.

C85F1046 - Shown are the 707B motor and optional Spicer 183 torque converter. This transmission had a starting ratio of 5 1/2 to 1, moving up automatically into direct drive as controlled by an adjustable governor. This transmission never achieved the acceptance of the Allison automatics, which were offered later.

The C model dash was very attractive and functional. An optional dash mounted tachometer is shown, as is the shift plate showing three positions: forward, neutral, and reverse. The torque converter transmission did not require a clutch pedal. The dash of a Mack 97D bus shows the similarity of the instrument cluster.

If you close your eyes, you can hear the lusty throb of the 707 motors, as FDNY pump tests five early C model pumpers.

C85F1049 1958 - Sayreville, NJ, received this closed cab pumper, which Mack called a canopy cab. The extra cost Federal Q siren is shown, as is the round Mack emblem on the cab and the cab front. The side mounting of this attractive emblem was very rare.

C85F1050/1 1958 - Mack never courted the aerial ladder market, particularly tillers, but received many orders nonetheless. FDNY took delivery of eleven C model Maxim 85-foot tillers in 1959 and thirteen more in 1960. The unit in this photo is a C85 tractor with a 100-foot Magirus aerial, one of two delivered in 1959.

C85F1080 1958 - This canopy cab for Larchmont, NY, had a roof mounted Federal Q siren, front suction, single air horn, deluxe turn signals, and extra grab handles in the pump panel area.

C85F1080 - Shown receiving water through the front suction inlet, two discharge lines are supplying the deck mounted deluge gun. Turnout gear was carried on the optional coat and boot rails.

C85F1077 1958 - Dumont, NJ, was scheduled to get the last of six cab-forward Ahrens-Foxes built, but cancelled the order, not wishing to own an "orphan." They later took delivery of this C85 with open cab, which Mack called a semi-cab. Numerous options shown are deluxe siren, arrow type turn signals, dual booster reels, dual coat and boot racks, individual pressure gauges, and windshield post mounted red lights and spot lights.

C85F-1090-359-F 7746

C85F1090 1959 - Not many fire trucks carry an advertising slogan on their side, but I suspect Valvoline may have made a substantial contribution toward the purchase of this unit. The siren was in the normal "between the headlights" position, and only compartments forward of the rear fenders were specified.

C85F1128 1959 - Elmont, NY's aerial featured 6-inch front red lights, deluxe turn signals, and dual sirens with red lights on the roof.

C85F1128 - A 75-foot Maxim ladder was used as well as aluminum ground ladders and extensive compartmentation.

C85F1091 1959 - Woodbourne, NY, specified larger than standard ladders, full side compartments, dual booster reels, roof mounted siren, front suction, and mud and snow tires.

C85FI129/30 1961 - Two of these unusual 146-foot, seven section Magirus ladders were mounted on C85 chassis for FDNY. They were eventually designated High Ladders One and Two, and were later refitted with 100-foot Grove ladders.

C85F1135-260-F8106

C85F1135 1960 - Long Island, NY, was fond of Mack apparatus. This North Babylon pumper had extra striping and an unusual 2 1/2-inch gated front hose connection.

C85FI139 1960 - One of the first rigs shown with "West Coast" mirrors was this canopy cab pumper. The ladders were higher than normal due to an extra compartment over the rear wheels.

C85F1147 1960 - An unusual angle shot of Oyster Bay, NY's aerial ladder. Extras shown are deluxe turn signals, windshield post red lights, inside and outside wipers, radio speaker, and mounted hand lights.

C85F-1161-760-F8331

C85F1161 1960 - This semi-cab for Avalon, NJ, featured an extra length of hard suction hose as well as a bell, which is no longer a standard item.

C85F-1166-860-F 8375

C85F1166 1960 - Marshall, TX, opted for the semi-cab, which was still very popular, although beginning to wane in popularity. Standard wood ladders and a single booster reel are shown.

C85F1170 1961 - Rescue bodies were rare on C units, but this Gerstenslager bodied rescue for West Hempstead, NY, is a fine example. Like many other Long Island departments, this one featured dual sirens and extra lighting and striping.

C85F-1176-1160-F8497

C85F1176 1960 - Baltimore County, MD, was a major Mack user. This pumper featured a canopy mounted deluge, extra hard suction hose, and an extended wheelbase. Waterous pumps have now replaced Hale, but it appears the discharge handles are of the Hale style.

C85F1179 1961 - Semi-cabs were popular on aerial ladders such as this unit, which featured a Federal Q siren, Mars light, bell, and side mounted booster reel. The list price of an 85-foot aerial in 1961 was $41,100, with a charge of $425 for a closed canopy cab.

C85F1196 1961 - This pumper for Rockford, IL, was unusual for several reasons. It had no lights or warning devices on the roof, had the older style Mack governor instead of a Waterous relief valve, and had no side compartments. The list price of a C85F pumper in 1961 was $21,200.

C85F1196 - Pump panel details included a gated 2 1/2-inch inlet and individual pressure gauges.

C85F1196 - Painted rear panels were standard. Options shown are a gated rear suction, 2 1/2-inch rear discharge, 1 1/2-inch discharge in hose compartment, extra hose bed partition, and extra large tail and stop lights.

C85F1200 1961 - This tiller tractor was destined for Richmond, VA, a long time Mack user. Many departments bought tractors only to upgrade older tillers, or in some cases, to replace wrecked tractors.

C85F1205 1961 - This pumper for Winkler County, Kermit, TX, had standard siren and 360 revolving red light and bumper mounted turn signals. Options were 6-inch front red lights, extra booster reel, and individual pressure gauges.

C85F1213 1962 - Long time Mack user, Lynbrook, NY, took delivery of this impressive tillered aerial. It was equipped with a 707C motor, Spicer 183 torque convertor, air brakes, and power steering.

C85F1243 1962 - This 85-foot aerial was well decked out with bell, West Coast mirrors, disc wheels, inside and outside wipers, and extra compartments. Allentown plant 5A is in the background.

C85F1291-1063C12668

C85F1291 1963 - The first Mack Aerialscope, aerial platform type device, was delivered in July 1964 to FDNY. It had a gasoline 707C motor and a 75-foot Truco boom. Dubbed "tower ladders" by FDNY, Mack delivered 171 more on both the C and CF chassis during the next 27 years.

C85F1294 1963 - Nevada, MO, received this rather standard equipped pumper, with the exception of the overhead ladder rack.

C85F1318 1964 - Danville, PA, received this pumper equipped with an electronic siren, dual reels, individual pressure gauges, extra hard suction hose, and mud and snow tires.

C85F1318 - Standard painting and striping, as well as standard tail lights and turn signals are shown. Options were the dual coat and boot rails and the marine type red warning lights. The 1 1/2-inch and 2 1/2-inch rear discharges were also options. Many F model highway trucks are shown in the background.

C85FD1349 1965 - As part of the New York Super Pumper System, Mack delivered three satellite hose tenders. These units were diesel powered with manual transmissions and had a hose bed for 2,000 feet of 4 1/2-inch hose. No pump was installed, but dual side mounted 4 1/2-inch intakes on each side fed the giant 4000 GPM Stang monitor.

C85FAP1371 1966 - This early Aerialscope for Massena, NY, was delivered with a 75-foot Eaton boom, bell, and electronic siren. Mack officials in the basket are (L to R) E. W. Brunner, Bill O'Hare, G. F. Jones, and J. J. Klein Jr.

C85FAP1373 1967 - Allentown, PA, received one of the twelve C model Aerialscopes built with the Eaton boom. Shown in the background are F and R model highway trucks.

TYPE 95

Type 95s were produced from 1957 through 1967 and were the best selling type with 605 produced. The first type 95 (C95F1001) was delivered to Blue Ash, OH, on March 10, 1960. It was possibly being used initially as a demonstrator. The final type 95 (C95FD1651) was delivered to Bladensburg, MD, on June 20, 1969. No explanation is given as to the long delay in delivery of this unit.

The type 95, like the 85, was equipped with 707B or 707C gasoline motors as standard, or the ENDTF673 diesel as an option after 1960.

A 1000 GPM, two stage centrifugal pump of Hale–then Waterous brand–was standard.

C95F1001 1958 - The first C95 off the line went to Blue Ash, OH. The most noteworthy item on this rig was the unusual siren bracket. Blue Ash had the distinction of operating the only stainless steel bodied pumper built by Mack. (See page 78 of *Mack Model CF Fire Trucks 1967 - 1981 Photo Archive*)

C95F1002 1958 - The second C95 built went to Winston-Salem, NC. It had a roof mounted siren, larger than standard ladders, and a booster reel mounting in the same manner as the initial large order of C85 pumpers for FDNY.

C95F1003 1958 - Typical of West Coast deliveries, this semi-cab pumper for Mt. Vernon, WA, featured a B&M CS8 siren and disc wheels.

C95F1005/16 1958 - In addition to the fifty-two C85 pumpers delivered in 1958, FDNY also received twelve C95s. Other than the larger pump, the only major difference from the C85 orders was the use of large 6-inch master pump gauges, which quickly gained acceptance with other departments, and became known in the field as "New York Gauges."

C95F1017 1958 - This all white pumper for Lapeer, MI had a roof mounted Federal Q siren, bell, extra discharge gauges, extra hard suction hose, dual booster reels, and an overhead ladder rack.

C95F1020-260-F8113

C95F1020 1960 - This canopy cab pumper for Locust Valley, NY was decked out with extra striping; chrome deck pipe; roof mounted beacon, air horn, and siren; low mounted spotlights; deluxe turn signals; 6-inch red front lights; side mounted booster reel; and front suction.

C95F1020 - This unit is "parade ready" with neatly packed hose beds and turnout gear. Options included concealed storage for suction hose and ladder, marine style red lights, deluxe turn signals, rear grab rail, rear discharge, extra rear step, and lower 1 1/2-inch hose compartment.

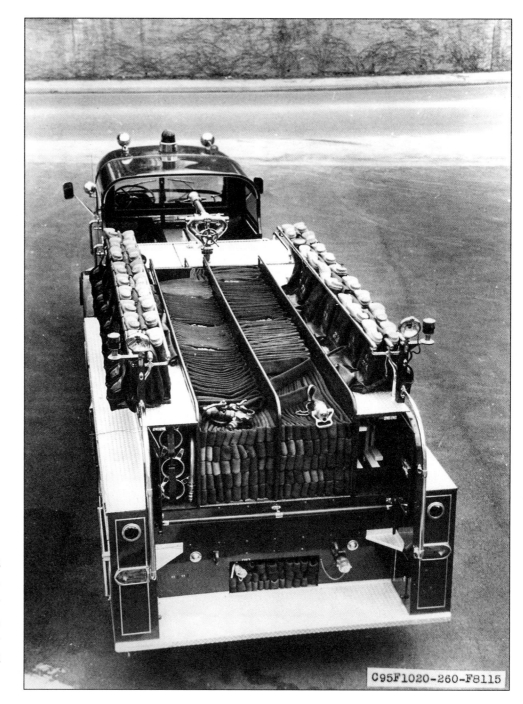

C95F1020-260-F8115

C95F1037 1959 - Lewisburg, PA's pumper sported a Federal Q siren, air horn, front suction, standard turn signals, and larger ladders. This unit is now privately owned.

C95F1047 1960 - One of the last C95s with a Hale pump was this semi-cab pumper for Cortland, NY. Disc wheels were fairly rare on East Coast rigs.

C95F1072 1960 - This semi-cab for San Clemente, CA, had a Waterous pump with Hale style discharge handles.

C95F1072 - Front end features included B&M siren, gated front suction, deluxe turn signals, and an enormous extended bumper with soft hose tray. The bumper mounted air horn was in an unusual location.

C95F-1063-1160-F8493

C95F1063 1960 - Quadruple combinations (pump, hose, booster, and long ladders), commonly called Quads, were very popular through the 1950s, but lost favor rapidly in the 1960s. This rare C model Quad for River Forest, IL, had a front suction with extended bumper, bumper mounted bell and Federal Q siren, and a Waterous pump with a Mack pressure governor.

C95F1102 1961 - Known for their sharp Mack equipment, Brandywine Hundred Fire Co. specified individual pressure gauges and an extended wheelbase.

C95F1106 1961 - This decked out pumper appears to be a nice companion piece to the Lynbrook, NY, aerial shown on page 61.

C95F1106 - Front end details included West Coast mirrors, deluxe turn signals, 6-inch red lights, Federal Q siren, gated front intake with preconnected soft suction hose, and an extended bumper with bell and suction strainer mounted. The rotating beacon light location indicates a low clearance fire house door opening.

C95F1106 - Rear end details included seats above the hose bed, extra red lights, four hose rollers, four hose bed compartments, and complete use of diamondette aluminum on rear hose body panel and beavertails.

C95F1156 1962 - One of the many Philly "Main Line" area fire companies buying Mack was Paoli, PA. This pumper cleared traffic with a Federal Q and dual cab mounted air horns. Mack plant 5A is in the background.

C95F1144/53 1962 - This 1962 order of ten pumpers to FDNY was still gasoline powered, but an additional C95 was delivered with a diesel motor–the first in the department. Beginning in 1965 all FDNY pumpers were equipped with diesels and automatic transmissions. Mack had always been the predominant supplier of motorized apparatus to FDNY, but the 1960s saw an even higher concentration of Mack units, which culminated in 1972 when every first line pumper in the department was a Mack.

ENGINE MODEL... **ENF 707C**

FOR MACK FIRE APPARATUS

THERMODYNE

———

GASOLINE

Dependable performance at lowest possible fuel and maintenance costs is the achievement of this powerful Mack gasoline engine.

Designed and manufactured exclusively for Mack Fire Apparatus, ENF 707C has been performance tested and time proven to be of outstanding dependability. A big engine with a piston displacement of 707 cubic inches, drivers find it quick to respond on the open highway and a dependable performer on steep grades.

The high power output and low fuel consumption of this engine is largely due to the highly-developed induction and exhaust systems, embodying dual downdraft carburetion and manifolds on opposite sides of the engine, with direct, straight

Right side showing air cleaner, oil filler, exhaust manifold, breather, air compressor, governor, two distributors and ignition coils and starting motor.

line passages to the valve ports and a large balancing port between inlet manifold sections to produce even distribution between the cylinders. The inlet manifold is water jacketed for uniform and rapid heating.

Mack quality features which insure long engine life include long water jackets for even and full cooling; sodium-mercury cooled exhaust valves; individual valve porting to avoid concentrations of heat; everlasting timing gears of the exclusive Mack drop-forged, case-hardened and generator-ground type; angle split connecting rod bearing caps permit easy removal of the rods through the cylinder bores; ample and scientific methods of lubrication.

Left side showing dual downdraft carburetor, water jacketed inlet manifold, oil filter, fuel pump and alternator. Auxiliary engine water cooler for pumper type Fire Apparatus only.

ENGINE MODEL ENF 707C
DETAIL SPECIFICATIONS

Make	Mack, Thermodyne
Number of cylinders	Six
Bore and stroke	5″ x 6″
A.M.A. horsepower	60.0
Maximum horsepower @ 2600 r.p.m.	276
Brake horsepower @ 2400 r.p.m. (gov.)	268
Piston displacement, cubic inches	707
Compression ratio	8.0
Max Torque @ 1400 r.p.m.	640 lb.-ft.
Cylinder block	Chromium-nickel iron
Cylinder heads cast in	Pairs
Pistons, material	Aluminum alloy
Piston rings, compression	Three
Oil Control	Two
Wristpin, type	Full-floating
Diameter	1-7/16″
Retention	Snap rings
Connecting rods, type	Drop-forged I-beam
Cap angle	35°
Length, center to center	11-1/4″
Crankshaft	Integral counterweights
Material	Medium carbon steel, Tocco hardened journals
Weight	216 lbs.
Vibration damper	Viscous type, torsional
Main bearings, material	Copper-lead, steel back, babbitt overlay
Number	Seven
Diameter	4″
Total length	10-29/64″
Connecting rod bearings	
Material	Copper-lead, steel back with babbitt overlay
Crankpins, dia. & length	3″ x 2¼″
Camshaft, bearings	Seven
Timing drive	Drop-forged, case-hardened, generator ground helical gears
Valve-lifter, type	Tungsten-carbide faced, mushroom
Exhaust valve seats	Permafit inserts of Niferrite (Nickel-cast iron, copper plated and faced with Stellite)

Valves, location	Overhead
Exhaust	Sodium-mercury cooled, hard faced, with positive type rotators
Clear diameter of ports,	
Inlet	2-1/16″
Exhaust	1-3/4″
Lift, Inlet & exhaust	0.500″
Material, Inlet	Silicon-chromium-nickel steel
Exhaust	Face, stellite, head and upper end of stem, silicon-nickel-chromium steel; lower end of stem nickel-chromium-molybdenum steel
Firing order	1-5-3-6-2-4
Ignition: (Double)	
Distributor, make	Delco-Remy
Advance	Full automatic
Spark plug, size	14 mm.
Carburetor, make and type	Zenith, dual downdraft
Model	29D14RP
Size	1-3/4″
Fuel Feed, type	Fuel pump, 6-valve (diaphragm) Electrical (on chassis frame)
Governor, make	Pierce
Type	Mechanical
Air Cleaner,	
Conventional Cab	Vortox, dry, wire-mesh type
Cab Forward	Airmaze, filter
Manifolds:	
Intake (left)	One-piece, six-port
Exhaust (right)	Three-piece, six-port
Cooling:	
Thermostat starts to open at 170°	
Water delivery to cylinder block	From pump to block through header core on right side of engine
To cylinder head	Through openings in header to directional tubes and thence to area between valve seats
Fan, type	Asymmetrical
Diameter	23″, five blades

*Auxiliary cooler—Pump water through copper coil in unit in thermostatically controlled by-pass system.
*Standard for Pumper type Fire Apparatus only.

Water capacity of system	55 quarts
Lubrication, oil filter:	
Make	W. G. B.
Type & capacity	By-pass, 2 quarts
Oil capacity, (including filter)	17 quarts
Alternator	12 volts, 100 Amps.
Starter	12 volts

The ENF707C was Mack's premium and largest fire apparatus motor. It was standard in the B and C types 85, 95, and 125. It had a sterling reputation for both performance and dependability. Mack introduced their diesel motor in fire apparatus in 1960. The 707C was used until 1973 when the last one was installed in a CF pumper.

C95F1224 1963 - This NJ semi-cab delivery included Mack West Coast mirrors, inside and outside wipers, folding roof ladder, and electronic siren.

C95FMD-1228-1163-F9748

C95FMD1228 1963 - One of the first C95s delivered with an ENDTF673 diesel motor was this canopy cab pumper for Cherry Hill, NJ. An extended wheelbase, side mounted booster reel, and higher than normal hose body are evident.

C95F1292 1964 - This delivery to Hatboro, PA, shows dual telescoping quartz lights and protective brightwork on the pump panel and forward edge of the hose body.

C95F1340 1965 - Hazleton, PA's pumper was equipped with both a mechanical and electronic siren.

C95F1349 1965 - Camp Hill, PA, was a "Mack company" for many years. Three options which were becoming increasingly popular were telescopic quartz lights, 45 degree discharge elbows, and a radio speaker grille in the front of the side compartment.

C95F1349 - Popular options were rear rubber covered grab rail, extra steps, and diamondette aluminum on rear of body and beavertails.

C95FD1363 1965 - Mt. Pleasant, PA, specified several options but stayed with the standard siren.

C95F1446 1966 - This Bangor, ME, pumper was appropriately photographed in snow, a condition it would operate in frequently when placed in service.

C95F1503 1966 - This Ogontz, PA, delivery displays the typical options frequently specified, except for the color, which was solid white.

C95F1579 1967 - One of the last C95s produced was this canopy cab pumper for Milton, PA. An unusual spec was the highway rig type cab clearance lights. This rig is now privately owned and frequently seen on the parade and muster circuits. Both R model and off highway rigs are seen in the background.

C95FD1587/90 1967 - Detroit, MI, received four C95 diesels in 1967. This was obviously shot at some type of show, although the officials are not identified. Information shown on the chart states rig has an ENDTF673B diesel, Spicer automatic transmission, air brakes, front suction, 300 gallon tank, and electric rewind booster reel.

This 1967 photo shows two of Detroit's C models "strutting their stuff" in a parade. A 70th anniversary Seagrave tiller is also shown. In the early 1960s, every first line pumper and ladder in Detroit was a Seagrave.

ENGINE MODEL . . . ENDTF 673

FOR MACK FIRE APPARATUS

TURBOCHARGED

THERMODYNE

DIESEL

For the choice of diesel, the Mack ENDTF 673 engine is an excellent fire apparatus powerplant. This diesel is specifically adapted and fitted for fire apparatus. The engine is TURBOCHARGED and develops a maximum horsepower of 230 at the moderate speed of 2300 RPM. Starting is reliably quick, the engine has the smoothness and flexibility for good roadability and the high endurance for long periods of continuous pumping.

The engine is of the open-chamber type with multiple-unit direct injection system operating at moderate pressure, high velocity air swirl and high capacity breathing — assets to thermal efficiency and fuel economy. Compared to the parent, naturally aspirated engine the TURBOCHARGED engine develops more horsepower by virtue of greater air charge. The TURBOCHARGER is centrifugal, turbine driven by the exhaust gases. Turbine and blower are in compact combination.

On the engine right side, in accessible arrangement are: the turbocharger, injection pump with governor, fuel filter, air compressor and starting motor.

There is no mechanical drive from the engine, no consumption of any engine power and the charger is oil cooled.

Among the recognized long-life and maintenance-reducing features of this Mack diesel are uniform cooling through directed water flow; fully-counter-balanced, induction case-hardened crankshaft with cool-running hollow crankpins and viscous vibration damper; angle-split connecting rods; cylinder heads in threes; dry cylinder liners, carboloy-faced valve lifters and Mack's exclusive Everlasting Timing Gears — drop-forged for strength, case-hardened for durability and generator-ground for quietness.

This engine provides diesel power of the highest order and perfectly adapted for fire fighting.

Left side view shows turbocharger connection to intake manifold, one of two lube oil filters, and simple, yet sturdy mounting of the generator affording easy adjustment of belt tension.

ENGINE MODEL ENDTF 673
DETAIL SPECIFICATIONS

Make	Mack, Thermodyne
Type	Diesel, Turbocharged
Number of cylinders	Six
Bore and stroke	4-7/8" x 6"
A.M.A. horsepower	57.0
Maximum horsepower @ 2300 r.p.m.	230
Brake horsepower, @ 2100 r.p.m. (gov.)	220
Piston displacement	672 cubic inches
Compression @ 1000 r.p.m.	425 lbs. per sq. in.
Compression ratio	15.5
Maximum Torque @ 1600 r.p.m.	590 lb.-ft.
Brake mean effective pressure @ 1600 r.p.m.	131 lbs. per sq. in.
Cylinder block	
Material	Chromium-nickel alloy iron
Cylinder sleeves	Special alloy iron phosphate coated
Type	Dry
Cylinder heads cast in	Threes
Pistons, material	Aluminum alloy
Piston rings, compression	Three (all chrome plated)
Oil control	Two (chrome plated)
Wristpin, type	Full-floating
Diameter	1-5/8"
Retention	Snap rings
Connecting rods, type	Drop-forged I-beam
Cap angle	35°
Length, center to center	11-1/4"
Crankshaft	Integral counterweights
Material	Medium carbon steel Tocco hardened journals
Weight	216 lbs.
Vibration damper	Viscous type
Main bearings, material	Copper-lead, steel back with babbitt overlay
Number and diameter	Seven, 4"
Total length	10-15/16"
Connecting rod bearings,	
Material	Copper-lead steel back with babbitt overlay
Crankpins, dia. & length	3" x 2-1/4"
Camshaft, bearings	Seven
Timing drive	Manganese steel, case hardened, generator ground helical gears
Valve lifter, type	Tungsten carbide faced, mushroom

Inlet and exhaust valve seats	Permafit inserts of Niferrite (nickel cast iron copper-plated and faced with Stellite)
Valves, exhaust	Hard faced, with positive type rotators
Location	Overhead
Clear dia. of ports, inlet	2-3/64"
Exhaust	1-11/16"
Lift, inlet and exhaust	9/16"
Material, inlet	Chromium-silicon steel
Exhaust	Stabl-ite (head and upper end of stem: chromium-nickel-nitrogen-austenitic steel; lower end of stem: nickel-chromium-molybdenum steel)
Firing order	1-5-3-6-2-4
Fuel injection pump, make	American Bosch
Type	Multiple unit, flange mounted
Transfer pump, type	Plunger
Nozzles, type	Four-hole spray
Governor, make	American Bosch
Type	Mechanical, with torque control
Air cleaner	Oil bath type
Capacity	4 quarts
Air Compressor (gear driven)	Tu-Flo 500 *Required for air brakes*
Turbocharger:	
Type	Exhaust gas driven, centrifugal
Mounting	Exhaust manifold flange
Lubrication	From engine
Cooling	From engine (oil)
Cooling:	
Water delivery to cylinder block	Through header cored in block
To cylinder head	From cylinder block through ports directed toward exhaust valve seats
Thermostat, starts to open	170°
Fan, type	Asymmetrical
Number of blades & dia.	Five; 23"
Drive	Two V-belts
Water capacity of system	44 quarts
Lubrication, Engine oil filter:	
Make and model	Luberfiner (272C) & Purolator
Type	By-pass / Full-flow
Capacity	4 quarts / 12 quarts
Engine oil cooler	American Standard (2 quarts)
Oil capacity, including filter and oil cooler	33 quarts
Alternator	12 Volt, 100 Amps.
Starter	24 Volts

Mack introduced their first diesel powered fire apparatus in 1960 with the delivery of three B model pumpers and hose wagons to Hamilton, Bermuda. Mack was convinced of the advantages of diesel power in the fire service and became the major supplier of diesel fire apparatus. In an effort to convince reluctant potential customers, Mack conducted a 24 hour demonstration in Chicago in 1963. This was so successful, Mack then conducted a full week pumping marathon in Detroit, MI. A Mack C95 pumper pumped a continuous 1000 GPM from noon of July 5, until noon of July 11, 1964, one full week without an engine shut-off.

Mack proudly proclaimed this C95 pumped 10,160,640 gallons on only 1,108 gallons of fuel during this non-stop 7 day Detroit marathon. Mack credited this record to the durability of the ENDTF673 motor and the simplicity of the diesel motor with less to go wrong. Mack stated the C95 consumed approximately 6.6 gallons of fuel per hour during the 7 day period and that a comparable gasoline motor would have consumed about 15 gallons of gasoline per hour under the same conditions. Not surprisingly, Mack diesels, as well as competitive makes, increased in popularity to the point where the gasoline motor is now only available and used in the smaller apparatus.

The Mack ENDTF673C, as widely used in both B and C model fire apparatus, is shown. As with the 707C gasoline motor, chrome valve covers were installed.

TYPE 125

Type 125s were produced from 1958 through 1967 with 129 built. The first three type 125s were delivered to Ottawa, Ontario, Canada (C125F1001 through 3), in late 1958. The last delivery (C125FD1136) was to El Monte, CA, on February 12, 1968.

The Mack 707B or 707C gasoline motor was standard, as was a 1250 GPM two stage centrifugal pump.

C125F1004/5 1958 - The fourth and fifth C125s built went to Cleveland, OH. A bell, individual pressure gauges, and an extra hard suction hose were supplied.

C125F1004/5 - Pump panel details included a Mack pressure governor, push button primer, a water temperature gauge, and reducers on the suction inlet.

C125F1011 1960 - This white pumper for Syracuse, NY, was equipped with red disc wheels.

C125F1032 1963 - A plumber's heaven or nightmare, depending on your point of view, describes this pump area.

C125FMD1033 1963 - This white diesel pumper for Augusta, GA, was equipped with West Coast mirrors, standard turn signals, a bell, and Waterous pump.

C125F1037 1964 - This East Paterson, NJ, pumper featured a front suction, bell, Federal Q siren, dual boosters, extra hard suction, and a chrome pump panel.

C125F1043/4 1964 - Major options on this Mt. Vernon, NY, pumper included front suction, bell, extra striping, and triple coat and boot rails.

C125FD1088 1966 - This Garfied, NJ, pumper has a diesel motor and an extended wheelbase. A Mack B model highway truck is in the background.

C125FD1113 1967 - One of the last C125s built is this diesel headed for Long Beach, CA. The characteristic West Coast siren is shown as well as red lights above the windshield. The side gated suction inlet is extremely unusual, and it appears soft suction hose will be stored in the forward compartment. An R model highway truck is in the background.

The following are photos of C models, both at rest and hard at work.

Waynesboro, PA, was a "Mack town," and four of their fleet are posed in front of the Always There Hook & Ladder Co. Shown are a semi and canopy cab C model, an E model, and a B model aerial.

Greenville, PA, poses their 1934 500 GPM pumper, 1961 C75 pumper, and 1966 C85 aerial ladder.

Glen Ridge, NJ's C model aerial is about to make a run. An E model is shown in the adjoining bay.

This Lapeer, MI, C95 makes a hydrant connection utilizing a rear suction intake.

Two white pumpers of the Milwaukee, OR, Rural Fire District are about to respond. The roof mount for the Federal Q siren was unusual.

A two tone pumper and aerial are working a drill.

Two Cs followed by a faithful old "L" are responding in Portsmouth, VA.

A lot of hard work lies ahead for this crew advancing a line off a pumper setting up a draft with three sections of hard suction hose in Portsmouth, VA.

A Richmond, VA, pumper responding. The "Esso" sign in the background dates this photo.

This Tulsa, OK, pumper is undergoing a pump test, with plenty of "pump panel jockeys" present.

Newark, NJ, pumper making a front suction hydrant hookup.

This shot was part of an ad in 1963 touting the new ENDT673 motor, in a cab-forward, canopy cab model, which Mack stated would soon overtake conventional, gasoline powered pumpers in all round popularity. They were right on both counts!

C-85F AERIAL LADDER TRUCK

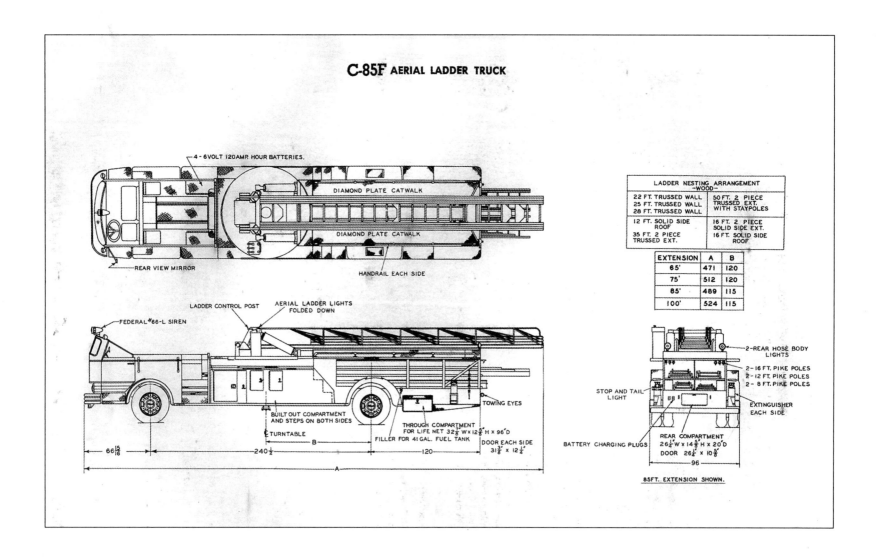

4 - 6 VOLT 120 AMP. HOUR BATTERIES.

DIAMOND PLATE CATWALK

DIAMOND PLATE CATWALK

REAR VIEW MIRROR

HANDRAIL EACH SIDE

LADDER NESTING ARRANGEMENT	
-WOOD-	
22 FT. TRUSSED WALL 25 FT. TRUSSED WALL 28 FT. TRUSSED WALL	50 FT. 2 PIECE TRUSSED EXT. WITH STAYPOLES
12 FT. SOLID SIDE ROOF 35 FT. 2 PIECE TRUSSED EXT.	16 FT. 2 PIECE SOLID SIDE EXT. 16 FT. SOLID SIDE ROOF

EXTENSION	A	B
65'	471	120
75'	512	120
85'	489	115
100'	524	115

LADDER CONTROL POST

AERIAL LADDER LIGHTS FOLDED DOWN

FEDERAL #66-L SIREN

2-REAR HOSE BODY LIGHTS

2-16 FT. PIKE POLES
2-12 FT. PIKE POLES
2- 8 FT. PIKE POLES

STOP AND TAIL LIGHT

EXTINGUISHER EACH SIDE

TOWING EYES

BUILT OUT COMPARTMENT AND STEPS ON BOTH SIDES

TURNTABLE

THROUGH COMPARTMENT FOR LIFE NET 32$\frac{1}{2}$ W x 12$\frac{5}{8}$ H x 96 D
FILLER FOR 41 GAL. FUEL TANK

DOOR EACH SIDE 31$\frac{3}{8}$ x 12$\frac{1}{4}$

BATTERY CHARGING PLUGS

REAR COMPARTMENT 26$\frac{1}{4}$ W x 14$\frac{3}{4}$ H x 20 D
DOOR 26$\frac{1}{4}$ x 10$\frac{3}{4}$

96

66$\frac{15}{16}$ 240$\frac{1}{2}$ B   120

A

85 FT. EXTENSION SHOWN.

More Titles from Iconografix:

AMERICAN CULTURE

AMERICAN SERVICE STATIONS 1935-1943 PHOTO ARCHIVE .... ISBN 1-882256-27-1
COCA-COLA: A HISTORY IN PHOTOGRAPHS 1930-1969 .... ISBN 1-882256-46-8
COCA-COLA: ITS VEHICLES IN PHOTOGRAPHS 1930-1969 .... ISBN 1-882256-47-6
PHILLIPS 66 1945-1954 PHOTO ARCHIVE .... ISBN 1-882256-42-5

AUTOMOTIVE

CADILLAC 1948-1964 PHOTO ALBUM .... ISBN 1-882256-83-2
CORVETTE THE EXOTIC EXPERIMENTAL CARS, LUDVIGSEN LIBRARY SERIES .... ISBN 1-58388-017-8
CORVETTE PROTOTYPES & SHOW CARS PHOTO ALBUM .... ISBN 1-882256-77-8
EARLY FORD V-8S 1932-1942 PHOTO ALBUM .... ISBN 1-882256-97-2
IMPERIAL 1955-1963 PHOTO ARCHIVE .... ISBN 1-882256-22-0
IMPERIAL 1964-1968 PHOTO ARCHIVE .... ISBN 1-882256-23-9
LINCOLN MOTOR CARS 1920-1942 PHOTO ARCHIVE .... ISBN 1-882256-57-3
LINCOLN MOTOR CARS 1946-1960 PHOTO ARCHIVE .... ISBN 1-882256-58-1
PACKARD MOTOR CARS 1935-1942 PHOTO ARCHIVE .... ISBN 1-882256-44-1
PACKARD MOTOR CARS 1946-1958 PHOTO ARCHIVE .... ISBN 1-882256-45-X
PONTIAC DREAM CARS, SHOW CARS & PROTOTYPES 1928-1998 PHOTO ALBUM .... ISBN 1-882256-93-X
PONTIAC FIREBIRD TRANS-AM 1969-1999 PHOTO ALBUM .... ISBN 1-882256-95-6
PORSCHE 356 1948-1965 PHOTO ALBUM .... ISBN 1-882256-85-9
STUDEBAKER 1933-1942 PHOTO ARCHIVE .... ISBN 1-882256-24-7
STUDEBAKER 1946-1958 PHOTO ARCHIVE .... ISBN 1-882256-25-5

EMERGENCY VEHICLES

AMERICAN LAFRANCE 700 SERIES 1945-1952 PHOTO ARCHIVE .... ISBN 1-882256-90-5
AMERICAN LAFRANCE 700 & 800 SERIES 1953-1958 PHOTO ARCHIVE .... ISBN 1-882256-91-3
AMERICAN LAFRANCE 900 SERIES 1958-1964 PHOTO ARCHIVE .... ISBN 1-58388-002-X
CLASSIC AMERICAN AMBULANCES 1900-1979 PHOTO ARCHIVE .... ISBN 1-882256-94-8
CLASSIC AMERICAN FUNERAL VEHICLES 1900-1980 PHOTO ARCHIVE .... ISBN 1-58388-016-X
FIRE CHIEF CARS 1900-1997 PHOTO ALBUM .... ISBN 1-882256-87-5
LOS ANGELES CITY FIRE APPARATUS 1953 - 1999 PHOTO ARCHIVE .... ISBN 1-58388-012-7
MACK® MODEL B FIRE TRUCKS 1954-1966 PHOTO ARCHIVE* .... ISBN 1-882256-62-X
MACK MODEL C FIRE TRUCKS 1957-1967 PHOTO ARCHIVE* .... ISBN 1-58388-014-3
MACK MODEL CF FIRE TRUCKS 1967-1981 PHOTO ARCHIVE* .... ISBN 1-882256-63-8
MACK MODEL L FIRE TRUCKS 1940-1954 PHOTO ARCHIVE* .... ISBN 1-882256-86-7
PIERCE ARROW FIRE APPARATUS 1979-1998 PHOTO ARCHIVE .... ISBN 1-58388-023-2
SEAGRAVE 70TH ANNIVERSARY SERIES PHOTO ARCHIVE .... ISBN 1-58388-001-1
VOLUNTEER & RURAL FIRE APPARATUS PHOTO GALLERY .... ISBN 1-58388-005-4

RACING

GT40 PHOTO ARCHIVE .... ISBN 1-882256-64-6
INDY CARS OF THE 1950s, LUDVIGSEN LIBRARY SERIES .... ISBN 1-58388-018-6
JUAN MANUEL FANGIO WORLD CHAMPION DRIVER SERIES PHOTO ALBUM .... ISBN 1-58388-008-9
LE MANS 1950: THE BRIGGS CUNNINGHAM CAMPAIGN PHOTO ARCHIVE .... ISBN 1-882256-21-2
LOTUS RACE CARS 1961-1994 PHOTO ALBUM .... ISBN 1-882256-84-0
MARIO ANDRETTI WORLD CHAMPION DRIVER SERIES PHOTO ALBUM .... ISBN 1-58388-009-7
SEBRING 12-HOUR RACE 1970 PHOTO ARCHIVE .... ISBN 1-882256-20-4
VANDERBILT CUP RACE 1936 & 1937 PHOTO ARCHIVE .... ISBN 1-882256-66-2
WILLIAMS 1969-1998 30 YEARS OF GRAND PRIX RACING PHOTO ALBUM .... ISBN 1-58388-000-3

RAILWAYS

CHICAGO, ST. PAUL, MINNEAPOLIS & OMAHA RAILWAY 1880-1940 PHOTO ARCHIVE ...... ISBN 1-882256-67-0
CHICAGO & NORTH WESTERN RAILWAY 1975-1995 PHOTO ARCHIVE .... ISBN 1-882256-76-X
GREAT NORTHERN RAILWAY 1945-1970 PHOTO ARCHIVE .... ISBN 1-882256-56-5
GREAT NORTHERN RAILWAY 1945-1970 VOL 2 PHOTO ARCHIVE .... ISBN 1-882256-79-4
MILWAUKEE ROAD 1850-1960 PHOTO ARCHIVE .... ISBN 1-882256-61-1
SOO LINE 1975-1992 PHOTO ARCHIVE .... ISBN 1-882256-68-9
TRAINS OF THE TWIN PORTS, DULUTH-SUPERIOR IN THE 1950s PHOTO ARCHIVE .... ISBN 1-58388-003-8
TRAINS OF THE CIRCUS 1872-1956 PHOTO ARCHIVE .... ISBN 1-58388-024-0
WISCONSIN CENTRAL LIMITED 1987-1996 PHOTO ARCHIVE .... ISBN 1-882256-75-1
WISCONSIN CENTRAL RAILWAY 1871-1909 PHOTO ARCHIVE .... ISBN 1-882256-78-6

TRUCKS & BUSES

BEVERAGE TRUCKS 1910-1975 PHOTO ARCHIVE .... ISBN 1-882256-60-3
BROCKWAY TRUCKS 1948-1961 PHOTO ARCHIVE* .... ISBN 1-882256-55-7
DODGE PICKUPS 1939-1978 PHOTO ALBUM .... ISBN 1-882256-82-4
DODGE POWER WAGONS 1940-1980 PHOTO ARCHIVE .... ISBN 1-882256-89-1
DODGE POWER WAGON PHOTO HISTORY .... ISBN 1-58388-019-4
DODGE TRUCKS 1929-1947 PHOTO ARCHIVE .... ISBN 1-882256-36-0
DODGE TRUCKS 1948-1960 PHOTO ARCHIVE .... ISBN 1-882256-37-9
THE GENERAL MOTORS NEW LOOK BUS PHOTO ARCHIVE .... ISBN 1-58388-007-0
JEEP 1941-2000 PHOTO ARCHIVE .... ISBN 1-58388-021-6
LOGGING TRUCKS 1915-1970 PHOTO ARCHIVE .... ISBN 1-882256-59-X
MACK MODEL AB PHOTO ARCHIVE* .... ISBN 1-882256-18-2
MACK AP SUPER-DUTY TRUCKS 1926-1938 PHOTO ARCHIVE* .... ISBN 1-882256-54-9
MACK BUSES 1900-1960 PHOTO ARCHIVE* .... ISBN 1-58388-020-8
MACK MODEL B 1953-1966 VOL 1 PHOTO ARCHIVE* .... ISBN 1-882256-19-0
MACK MODEL B 1953-1966 VOL 2 PHOTO ARCHIVE* .... ISBN 1-882256-34-4
MACK EB-EC-ED-EE-EF-EG-DE 1936-1951 PHOTO ARCHIVE* .... ISBN 1-882256-29-8
MACK EH-EJ-EM-EQ-ER-ES 1936-1950 PHOTO ARCHIVE* .... ISBN 1-882256-39-5
MACK FC-FCSW-NW 1936-1947 PHOTO ARCHIVE* .... ISBN 1-882256-28-X
MACK FG-FH-FJ-FK-FN-FP-FT-FW 1937-1950 PHOTO ARCHIVE* .... ISBN 1-882256-35-2
MACK LF-LH-LJ-LM-LT 1940-1956 PHOTO ARCHIVE* .... ISBN 1-882256-38-7
MACK TRUCKS PHOTO GALLERY* .... ISBN 1-882256-88-3
NEW CAR CARRIERS 1910-1998 PHOTO ALBUM .... ISBN 1-882256-98-0
PLYMOUTH COMMERCIAL VEHICLES PHOTO ARCHIVE .... ISBN 1-58388-004-6
STUDEBAKER TRUCKS 1927-1940 PHOTO ARCHIVE .... ISBN 1-882256-40-9
STUDEBAKER TRUCKS 1941-1964 PHOTO ARCHIVE .... ISBN 1-882256-41-7
WHITE TRUCKS 1900-1937 PHOTO ARCHIVE .... ISBN 1-882256-80-8

TRACTORS & CONSTRUCTION EQUIPMENT

CASE TRACTORS 1912-1959 PHOTO ARCHIVE .... ISBN 1-882256-32-8
CATERPILLAR PHOTO GALLERY .... ISBN 1-882256-70-0
CATERPILLAR POCKET GUIDE THE TRACK-TYPE TRACTORS 1925-1957 .... ISBN 1-58388-022-4
CATERPILLAR D-2 & R-2 PHOTO ARCHIVE .... ISBN 1-882256-99-9
CATERPILLAR D-8 1933-1974 INCLUDING DIESEL 75 & RD-8 PHOTO ARCHIVE .... ISBN 1-882256-96-4
CATERPILLAR MILITARY TRACTORS VOLUME 1 PHOTO ARCHIVE .... ISBN 1-882256-16-6
CATERPILLAR MILITARY TRACTORS VOLUME 2 PHOTO ARCHIVE .... ISBN 1-882256-17-4
CATERPILLAR SIXTY PHOTO ARCHIVE .... ISBN 1-882256-05-0
CATERPILLAR TEN INCLUDING 7C FIFTEEN & HIGH FIFTEEN PHOTO ARCHIVE .... ISBN 1-58388-011-9
CATERPILLAR THIRTY 2ND ED. INC. BEST THIRTY, 6G THIRTY & R-4 PHOTO ARCHIVE ...... ISBN 1-58388-006-2
CLETRAC AND OLIVER CRAWLERS PHOTO ARCHIVE .... ISBN 1-882256-43-3
ERIE SHOVEL PHOTO ARCHIVE .... ISBN 1-882256-69-7
FARMALL CUB PHOTO ARCHIVE .... ISBN 1-882256-71-9
FARMALL F- SERIES PHOTO ARCHIVE .... ISBN 1-882256-02-6
FARMALL MODEL H PHOTO ARCHIVE .... ISBN 1-882256-03-4
FARMALL MODEL M PHOTO ARCHIVE .... ISBN 1-882256-15-8
FARMALL REGULAR PHOTO ARCHIVE .... ISBN 1-882256-14-X
FARMALL SUPER SERIES PHOTO ARCHIVE .... ISBN 1-882256-49-2
FORDSON 1917-1928 PHOTO ARCHIVE .... ISBN 1-882256-33-6
HART-PARR PHOTO ARCHIVE .... ISBN 1-882256-08-5
HOLT TRACTORS PHOTO ARCHIVE .... ISBN 1-882256-10-7
INTERNATIONAL TRACTRACTOR PHOTO ARCHIVE .... ISBN 1-882256-48-4
INTERNATIONAL TD CRAWLERS 1933-1962 PHOTO ARCHIVE .... ISBN 1-882256-72-7
JOHN DEERE MODEL A PHOTO ARCHIVE .... ISBN 1-882256-12-3
JOHN DEERE MODEL B PHOTO ARCHIVE .... ISBN 1-882256-01-8
JOHN DEERE MODEL D PHOTO ARCHIVE .... ISBN 1-882256-00-X
JOHN DEERE 30 SERIES PHOTO ARCHIVE .... ISBN 1-882256-13-1
MINNEAPOLIS-MOLINE U-SERIES PHOTO ARCHIVE .... ISBN 1-882256-07-7
OLIVER TRACTORS PHOTO ARCHIVE .... ISBN 1-882256-09-3
RUSSELL GRADERS PHOTO ARCHIVE .... ISBN 1-882256-11-5
TWIN CITY TRACTOR PHOTO ARCHIVE .... ISBN 1-882256-06-9

*This product is sold under license from Mack Trucks, Inc. Mack is a registered Trademark of Mack Trucks, Inc. All rights reserved.

All Iconografix books are available from direct mail specialty book dealers and bookstores worldwide, or can be ordered from the publisher. For book trade and distribution information or to add your name to our mailing list contact:

Iconografix, PO Box 446, Hudson, Wisconsin, 54016   Telephone: (715) 381-9755, (800) 289-3504 (USA), Fax: (715) 381-9756

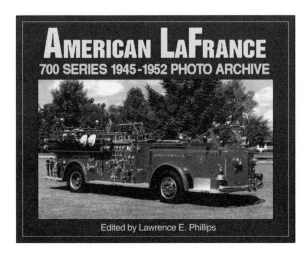
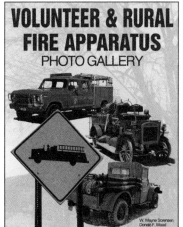
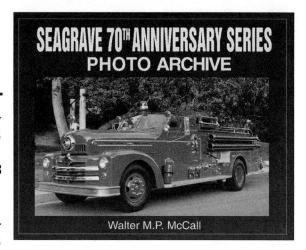
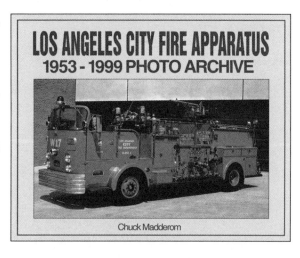
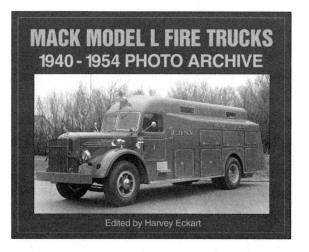